WHISTLER

CROWN PUBLISHING INC. - NEW YORK

WHISTLER

PIERRE CABANNE

Title page:
Portrait of the Artist With a Hat, 1857-1858
Oil on canvas, 46.3 × 38.1 cm (18$\frac{1}{4}$" × 15")
The Freer Gallery of Art, Smithsonian Institution, Washington, D.C.

Series published under the direction of:
Madeleine Ledivelec-Gloeckner

Translated from the French by:
Nicholas Max Jennings

Layout by:
Marie-Hélène Agüeros

Library of Congress Cataloging in Publication Data

Cabanne, Pierre.
    Whistler.

    Bibliography: pp. 94-95
    1. Whistler, James McNeill, 1834-1903.   2. Artists-
United States-Biography.   I. Title.
N6537.W4C33   1985   760'.092'4 [B]   85-9993
ISBN: 0-517-884119

10 9 8 7 6 5 4 3 2 1

First Paperback Edition

Printed in Italy - Poligrafiche Bolis S.P.A., Bergamo
© 1994 - Bonfini Press Establishment, Vaduz, Liechtenstein

Published by Crown Trade Paperbacks, 201 East 50th Street, New York,
New York 10022. Member of the Crown Publishing Group.

Random House, Inc. New York, Toronto, London, Sydney, Auckland

CROWN TRADE PAPERBACKS and colophon are trademarks of
Crown Publishers, Inc. Originally published in hardcover by
Crown Publishers, Inc. in 1985.

Nocturne in Blue and
Silver: Cremorne Lights
1872
Oil on canvas
50.2 × 70.3 cm
(19¾" × 29¼")
The Tate Gallery, London
Bequest of Arthur Studd

AN AMERICAN COMES TO PAINTING

James Abbott McNeill Whistler was a stylist — in life, in letters, and in painting. With his keen eye for publicity and his emphatic manner, he cut a spectacular figure in his championship of "new painting". It is best to picture the painter standing next to his work, armed with his paintbrush, his sharp sensitivity, and his gift for the peppery invective, as well as for the poetic turn of phrase — his most famous polemic is entitled "The Gentle Art of Making Enemies." He appears as one of the first modern painters. In many respects, he is a precursor figure. In his own day he was even forced to bear some of the badges of martyrdom. He shared with the Impressionists the honor of rejection by the Salon and violent attacks from the critics. His belated recognition came from a country other than his own. He was a member of the intellectual avant-garde of his time, a friend of Charles Baudelaire and Stéphane Mallarmé, of Gustave Courbet and Dante Gabriel Rossetti, of Count Robert de Montesquiou and Oscar Wilde. His *Nocturnes* provided inspiration for Claude Debussy's music, and he was one of the models for the painter Elstir in Marcel Proust's novel.

After his death in 1903, Whistler's reputation underwent a long eclipse. Perhaps Whistler was deprived of some of the attention of posterity because he did not struggle with poverty or display the mental anguish that turns the artist into a hero.   The critics accept artists who achieve the highest honors, but they can be unforgiving of those who merely enjoy worldly success and a ready, fashionable audience.   It was unfortunate that Whistler was never able to shed the image of the dandy.   Whether good-natured or proud, Edouard Manet, Edgar Degas, Auguste Renoir, and Paul Cézanne cut figures more familiar to the bourgeoisie, who could identify with them, with their circumstances, their families, their bearing, and even their dress.   Quite apart from his mannerisms and his provocative behavior, Whistler, with his ample mane of black hair in which a white forelock stood out, his monocle held by a broad silk ribbon, his piercing eyes, his slender, defiant profile, appeared like a musketeer who had adopted an American accent for exotic effect.   He had the reputation of being difficult.   Such a reputation can harm an artist, unless, as was the case with Degas, or later with the writer Paul Léautaud, such behavior conceals some inner tragedy, a bitter loneliness, and an uncompromising commitment to art itself.

Whistler was born an American — in 1834, in Lowell, Massachusetts — but he spent the greater part of his life in London and regarded himself as a Parisian.   This reflects another oddity in his character, which may be summed up as an evasiveness in the face of binding commitments.   This restless man was in constant search of a personal voice somewhere between pure creation and an elegant style, which was so pleasing to his vain and decadent friend Count Montesquiou and to Proust.   The latter, after attending the 1905 Whistler retrospective exhibition, went into ecstasies over "Venice in turquoise, Amsterdam in topaz, and Britanny in opal".   The technical demands and aesthetic preoccupations of Claude Monet and Cézanne would not have moved him so.   From there to say that Whistler's art belonged to the world of letters — the world of Mallarmé, who translated his "Ten O'Clock" lecture into French, of Oscar Wilde, Edmond de Goncourt, who was actually more sarcastic than admiring, J.-K. Huysmans, Henry James, Montesquiou, and Proust — there would be only one step.   But this would be going too far, even though he was indeed adopted by the Symbolist writers.   Whistler was attracted by Symbolism, fascinated as he was by everything that could suggest a world other than the one he lived in.   He loved the dreamlike quality, the contrived mannerism, and spiritual preoccupations of Symbolist literature and music.   He found the Symbolists more modern than the Impressionists, who were too naturalistic for his taste.   He shared with them a preference for decorative effects derived from the design and composition of Japanese prints, thus meeting the preoccupations of the English Pre-Raphaelites and announcing those of Art Nouveau.   Whistler defined modern art as a homage to Beauty — to a powerful and superior mastery that he worshipped with all his fervor, and to which he brought his rich sensitivity, his disdain for anything vulgar, and his search for a certain quality in art.   Art was to be dreamlike, magical, poetically suggestive, the antithesis of labor.

In any recollection of Whistler's life, it is difficult to overlook the position occupied by his friend Robert de Montesquiou, whose dubious reputation still casts a shadow over Whistler's.[1]   He gave Whistler moral support (if that is the word) in his determination to be above the rabble.   He held the dangerous idea that art and taste are essentially one and the same thing.   He was almost as famous in his day as Whistler for improbable and provocative sallies.   He certainly contributed to Whistler's reputation as a social butterfly, which clung as much to his art as to his person.   Whistler accepted that label, but it is worth looking a little deeper.

1. Montesquiou, himself a poet and a writer, was an admirer of Gustave Moreau. He probably was a model for Baron de Charlus in Proust's "Remembrance of Things Past" and for Des Esseintes in Huysman's "A Rebours". He introduced Whistler into fashionable Parisian society.

Twilight in Opal
Trouville, 1865
Oil on canvas
35 × 46 cm (13¾" × 18⅛")
The Toledo Museum of Art
Toledo, Ohio. Gift of
Florence Scott Libbey

Whistler was born into a long-established American family of Scottish and Irish descent. His father, George Washington Whistler, was a successful engineer, a graduate of West Point, who could himself be regarded as the prototype of the cultured Yankee globe-trotter. His mother, Anna Matilda McNeill, was George Washington Whistler's second wife. She was a Southerner and a devout Protestant. Her importance in Whistler's life is vouched by the fact that he added her surname, McNeill, to his name. Through his family, he belonged to a provincial, military, and puritanical tradition, hence his touchiness on points of honor, his ironical and sometimes brash wit, his feeling that he belonged to an imaginary order of chivalry. This created a somewhat anachronistic, idealized vision of the world and of men that was to express itself in his paintings. He was a headstrong man, full of racial prejudices that were eventually subdued by time, and while he had many mistresses and flaunted a fashionable hatred of women, he was of a perverse ambiguity and an exhibitionism characteristic of the times.

James had an older sister, Deborah, from his father's previous marriage, and a younger brother, William. In 1837 his family left Lowell for Stonington, Connecticut, where his father supervised the building of a railway. Later they settled in Springfield, Massachusetts, and in 1843 they left for Russia, where his father was to help build the railway between Moscow and St. Petersburg. There Whistler lived in the lap of luxury surrounded by household servants. He has a private tutor and took lessons in drawing and French. Later he took classes in drawing at the imperial Academy of Sciences, where he was noticed for his talent.

In 1847 and 1848 he visited his sister Deborah, who had been living in England since her marriage to Francis Seymour Haden, a surgeon and a skilled engraver. In London, Sir William Boxall painted his portrait, which was exhibited at the Royal Academy of Arts in 1849. This completed Whistler's conversion: He wrote to his father in St. Petersburg that he wanted to become a painter. His father, however, died very shortly afterward. Whistler's family returned to the

A Street at Saverne, 1858
Etching, II/V
20.8 × 15.7 cm
(8 1/16" × 6 3/16")
The Freer Gallery of Art
Smithsonian Institution
Washington, D.C.

United States, suffering from acute financial difficulties. He agreed to become a cadet at West Point, but it quickly became apparent that he was not suited for a military career. In 1853 he was dismissed because of his poor academic record (only in drawing was he at the top of his class). Friendly connections found him a job in the drawing division of the U.S. Coast and Geodetic Survey Office, where he etched maps and topographical plans. However, he did not like working for the Coast Survey Office and he was soon dismissed. Having read Henri Murger's "Scenes from Bohemian Life", which portrayed the life — particularly exotic when seen from America — of art students and working girls in Paris, he pleaded with his family to let him go and lead that carefree life in Paris. On November 3, 1855, Whistler arrived in Paris, with an allowance of three hundred-and-fifty dollars from his family, and he never again set a foot in the United States.

BETWEEN THE PRE-RAPHAELITES AND COURBET

This is how Whistler was remembered in 1905 by the painter and essayist Jacques-Emile Blanche — a bad painter but a very good essayist: "Among my earliest memories, I still remember the name of Whistler being bandied about by the men who posed for Fantin-Latour, next to Manet and in front of Delacroix's portrait. At the back of the artist's studio in the Rue des Beaux-Arts one could see the *Homage to Delacroix*, in which a slim, dandified figure squeezed into his long frock coat, with a white forelock standing out against curly black hair, a monocle, and an ironic mouth, turned toward the viewer. [...] This curious character intrigued me for a long time. [...] In his day, this 'Young Whistler' was an unconventional type of American. [...] He quickly vanished from the scene after a promising start."[2] That judgment was superficial and a little premature. Just a few months before Henri Fantin-Latour painted his *Homage to Delacroix*,[3] Baudelaire wrote a critical notice of some prints by Whistler in an unsigned article which first appeared in the April 2, 1862, issue of "Revue anecdotique" and was reprinted in the "Boulevard" five months later: "Just the other day a young American artist, Mr. Whistler, was showing at the Galerie Martinet, a set of etchings, subtle, lively as to their improvisation and inspiration, representing the banks of the Thames; wonderful tangles of rigging, yardarms and rope, a hotchpotch of fog, furnaces and corkscrews of smoke; the profound and intricate poetry of a vast capital."[4]

Whistler settled in Paris in 1855. The following year he joined the studio of a Swiss painter, Charles Gleyre, who specialized in ponderous allegorical and mythological scenes. He immediately took to the Bohemian life he had been looking for in Paris. His eccentric clothes, his restlessness, his turbulent affairs — one of his mistresses was known as "The Tigress" in the Latin Quarter — and his character, which oscillated between venom and affability, quickly set him among the dandies of Paris. In order to earn some money, he accepted commissions to copy works at the Musée du Luxembourg and at the Louvre. There he particularly admired Velázquez, whom he had already discovered at the Hermitage and whose work he went to see in Manchester at the 1857 Art Treasures Exhibition.[5] When Whistler was short of money he went to stay with his sister's family in London, which enabled him to visit the National Gallery and other British museums. It was also during this period that Félix Bracquemond introduced him to the art of the Japanese print, which proved to be a decisive influence.

2. Jacques-Emile Blanche. *De David à Degas*. Paris, 1927.

3. 1864, Musée d'Orsay, Paris.

4. Charles Baudelaire. *Art in Paris, 1845-1862*. Trans. by Jonathan Mayne. London: Phaidon, 1965, p. 220.

5. The exhibition included fourteen paintings by or attributed to Velázquez.

9

In October 1858, Whistler published his first series of engravings after an etching tour of Luxembourg, Alsace, and the Rhineland, which he dedicated to his brother-in-law, Seymour Haden, who had helped him to perfect his craft during his visits to England. He gave the series the title *Twelve Etchings From Nature* (it is also known as *The French Set*). These etchings were printed in Paris by Auguste Delâtre, the printer of the Barbizon painters, and published in London the following year. They depict various landscapes and local figures, but they also include a glimpse of the lovely Fumette — whose real name was Héloïse

— the "Tigress of the Latin Quarter". As Katharine Lochan puts it in her catalogue: "At first the selection appears to be random, and it is neither 'French' nor a 'Set' in conventional terms. [...] The chief sources of inspiration which lay behind it were to be found in the avant-garde artistic and intellectual circles in Paris, of which Whistler had become a part. [...] In selecting and mixing at random portraits of children, friends, the urban working poor, and urban and

"En Plein Soleil", 1858
Etching, II/II
10.1 × 13.3 cm
(3 ⅞" × 5 ¼")
The Metropolitan Museum of Art, New York
Harris Brisbane Dick Fund

rural genre, Whistler demonstrated his awareness of the direction in which French art was heading after the Salon of 1857. He selected for inclusion not the most consistent group of etchings which he had made to date, but those which demonstrated the virtuosity of his realist repertoire."[6]

6. Katharine A. Lochan. *The Etchings of James McNeill Whistler.* New Haven, London: Yale University Press, 1984, pp. 57-58.

It was Delâtre who engaged Whistler to find antique paper for his prints. Whistler developed a preference for creamy eighteenth-century Dutch laid rag paper, as well as for *japon mince*, a thin, almost transparent sheet of Oriental paper made

Finette, 1859
Drypoint, IX/X
28.8 × 20.1 cm
(11 ⅜" × 7 ⅞")
The New York Public Library
Astor, Lenox and Tilden
Foundations

from the bark of the mulberry tree. Many prints were pulled on *chine collé*, thin sheets of Japanese paper mounted on to larger sheets of machine-made wove paper. Delâtre had studied the chiaroscuro in Rembrandt's prints and he taught Whistler how to achieve different lighting effects by changing the color and amount of ink he put on the plates.

At the same time, Whistler made the acquaintance of Fantin-Latour, who was copying Veronese's *Wedding Feast at Cana* at the Louvre. They were both admirers of Courbet and this brought them together. Fantin-Latour introduced Whistler to the group of the Realists meeting at the Café Molière, some of whose members appear in *Homage to Delacroix*. Whistler became interested in the theory developed by Fantin-Latour's teacher, Paul Lecoq de Boisbaudran, on training one's visual memory. A meticulous and boring teacher, Lecoq claimed that if you looked deeply and attentively at things, you would be able to depict them faithfully from memory. Lecoq's course at the Ecole des Beaux-Arts was ill-attended, while Gleyre's was sought after because of the atmosphere of freedom that prevailed there.[7] However, it was Thomas Couture, despite his self-important manner, who had the most success. His sarcastic remarks about Eugène Delacroix did not deter Manet from going to pay his respects to the master, who

Venus, 1859
Etching, II/II
15.2 × 22.9 cm (6" × 9")
The Freer Gallery of Art
Smithsonian Institution
Washington, D.C.

7. Gleyre was known for giving his students a solid grounding and he encouraged them to find their own personal style. There was no tuition fee; students needed to pay only for the rental of the studio and the models. His school became a haven for young and needy artists of an independent mind.

8. Musée d'Orsay, Paris.

9. Léonce Bénédite. *L'Œuvre de James McNeill Whistler*. Paris, 1905.

was then in old age and rather distant despite his fame. Fantin-Latour later took Whistler to Delacroix's studio at the Place Furstenberg. Both Manet and Whistler can be seen on either side of the aged master in *Homage to Delacroix*.

That winter, Whistler did an excellent sketch of Fantin-Latour drawing while lying in bed with all his clothes on and wearing a scarf and top hat because of the cold.[8] It is an amusing snapshot, with the caption: "Fantin in bed engaged in his studies, having difficulties." At the time, noted Léonce Bénédite, Whistler admired his friend for his "simplicity and breadth" as well as for "the fresh vivid colors which are his specialty."[9]

What was he painting at the time? His earliest painting is *The Artist's Niece*, which dates from 1849.[10] Annie Harriet Haden, the daughter of his sister Deborah, was then about one year old. A few other portraits and landscapes from the period 1850-1855 are known to have disappeared, but one surviving painting is *Portrait of the Artist Smoking*, probably produced soon after Whistler's arrival in Paris in 1855. Of all the copies he made in the Louvre and the Musée du Luxembourg, only his version of Jean-Dominique Ingres's *Ruggiero*

10. Hunterian Art Gallery, University of Glasgow.

Liberating Angelica survives. Other paintings are a *Portrait of a Peasant Woman* (1855-1858),[11] which is very thickly painted, with sharp contrasts of light and shadow; an *Interior*, two portraits of *La Mère Gérard*, probably from 1858-1859. Finally, there is the *Portrait of Whistler With a Hat*,[12] in which the critic Théodore Duret detected "the influence of Rembrandt, with whom he had an infatuation at the time" — particularly *Head of a Young Man*, then but no longer attributed to Rembrandt, presumably showing his son Titus with long, curly hair and a broad, floppy beret. In 1859 Whistler painted *Brown and Silver: Old Battersea Bridge*.[13] It anticipates the painter's favorite themes

At the Piano, 1858
Oil on canvas
67 × 91 cm
(26⅜" × 36⅛")
The Taft Museum
Cincinnati, Ohio. Bequest
of Louise Taft Semple

and preoccupations. The theme is handled with broad brushstrokes and an attractive delicacy of execution, but without the inventive freedom which the subject later inspired in him.

In November 1858, when Whistler was staying with the Hadens on one of his trips to London, he convinced his sister Deborah and her daughter Annie to pose for *At the Piano*. Every time he came to stay, his sister tried to keep him in London for good, but he was enjoying life in Paris too much to accept. At the

The Lime-Burner, 1859
Etching and drypoint, I/II
25.1 × 17.6 cm
(9⅞" × 6¹⁵⁄₁₆")
The Freer Gallery of Art
Smithsonian Institution
Washington, D.C.

11. Hunterian Art Gallery, University of Glasgow.

12. See title page.

13. Addison Gallery of American Art, Andover, Massachusetts.

time, a serious artistic career could only be established in Paris. In January 1859 he brought *At the Piano* to Paris. It is a well-composed work and not unlike the intimist interiors done by Fantin-Latour at the same time. It should also be compared with Degas's *Bellelli Family* of 1860-1862, in which the bold composition shows a complete departure from portraits of academic tradition, and the figures are placed and represented as seen in real life.[14] Whistler's *At the Piano* is tame in comparison, but the harmony of white, greenish gray, and grayish ocher is full of studied refinement and contrasts with the large, flat surfaces of Deborah's black and Annie's white dresses and the maroon of the carpet. The only true innovation in the picture, but a significant one, is the fact that the prints lining the walls are cut off at a quarter of their height in a manner inspired by

14. Musée d'Orsay, Paris.

Rotherhithe
1860
Etching, II/III
27.5 × 19.9 cm
(10 ¼" × 7 ¾")
The New York Public Library
Astor, Lenox and Tilden
Foundations

Harmony in Green and Rose
The Music Room, 1860-1861
Oil on canvas
95.5 × 70.8 cm
(37 ⅝" × 27 ⅞")
The Freer Gallery of Art
Smithsonian Institution
Washington, D.C.

The Thames in Ice
1861
Oil on canvas
74.6 × 55.3 cm
(29⅜" × 21¾")
The Freer Gallery of Art
Smithsonian Institution
Washington, D.C.

Wapping on Thames
1861-1864
Oil on canvas
72.3 × 102.2 cm
(28½" × 40¼")
National Gallery of Art
Washington, D.C.
J.H. Whitney Collection

Japanese prints.   Such a mixture of traditionalism and innovation was characteristic of the experiments of the young Realists, but the Academy did not appreciate them at all.   *At the Piano* was rejected by the Salon of 1859, as were the entries by Fantin-Latour, Alphonse Legros, and Théodule Ribot, who were likewise guilty of allegiance to Courbet.   Another follower of Courbet, François Bonvin, put forward the suggestion that some of the rejected entries should be exhibited at his studio at the Rue Saint-Jacques.   He invited Courbet himself to the show, and Courbet was especially struck by Whistler's contribution, on which he warmly congratulated him.   The exhibition attracted a number of young painters to whom the portrayal of contemporary life was no less important than the new emphasis on color, its contrasts and subtle gradations, in preference to line.   The interest that Courbet showed in him made such a deep impression on Whistler that he went on a pilgrimage to Ornans, where the great man had grown up and drawn the inspiration for his major paintings.   However, the rejection of *At the Piano* by the Salon made him feel bitter about Paris, and he decided to leave in the spring of 1860 for London, where he set up house at Rotherhithe, next to the Thames, which figures so largely in his work.   Immediately, he addresses himself to the task of persuading his friends to come to London, as if simply by virtue of his presence London had become the artistic center of the world.   "England is

the country which welcomes young artists with open arms," he wrote to Fantin-Latour. The latter allowed himself to be persuaded, followed by Legros and Elie Delaunay, a nephew of Benjamin Constant, whose negligence in matters of dress did not endear him to the Hadens. Whistler was wrong about London. The art scene there was less lively and revolutionary than in Paris. By the time he settled in London, the great days of the Pre-Raphaelite Brotherhood were over. The group had been viewed as the English counterpart of the French Realist movement and its works had received praise from Baudelaire when they were shown at the Paris World Fair in 1855. They championed faithfulness to nature, a return to the purity of Italian painting before what they saw as the decadence born from Raphael's idealism, a departure from the excesses of academic style, and the spreading of an artistic culture among the working classes. In spite of their nostalgic tones and mannered style, the controversy which surrounded the first appearance of their work, their anti-academic stance, and their search for spirituality would have been sufficient to attract Whistler's attention. When he went to the Royal Academy exhibition together with Fantin-Latour, to admire John Millais's new work, Millais told him how much he liked his etchings, just as he was later to praise *At the Piano* when it was shown at the 1860 Royal Academy exhibition. The painting which had been rejected in Paris was given a warm reception in London. Everyone admired it and the painter John Philip, a friend of Millais's, bought it for thirty pounds. Deborah Haden was delighted that her brother had at last taken her advice, and the young American who had been denied recognition in Paris was becoming a highly regarded painter in England.

Whistler continued to do a lot of etchings, some of which were exhibited in Paris in 1862, but they were not published as a set before 1871, as a series of clear and firm depictions of the Thames entitled *Sixteen Etchings of Scenes on the Thames and Other Subjects*, the so-called *Thames Set*. Started in 1860, the painting *Wapping on Thames* [15] — in which Whistler's new model and mistress, Joanna Hiffernan, a red-haired Irish beauty, makes her first appearance — reveals a sense of atmosphere and light that is not far removed from Monet's and Frédéric Bazille's ideas of the same period: combining Realism with the immediacy of "plein-air" painting. [16]

In September 1861, Whistler left for France and in November he moved back to Paris with Jo, settling in the Boulevard des Batignolles, where he painted her as the subject of his *Symphony in White No. 1. The White Girl*. [17] The picture shows the young woman, standing on a bearskin rug and wearing a white dress, against a white background. In his catalogue, David Park Curry compares it to Antoine Watteau's *Gilles*: [18] a lonely figure in the foreground, somewhat flattened and uncomfortably silhouetted against its background, in a striking study of light playing over a model clad in white. [19] The flower she holds in her hand evokes Rossetti and the Pre-Raphaelite movement, and the restrained opulence of the painting reflects Whistler's admiration for Velázquez and the Spanish masters of the Golden Age. Yet the painting was rejected by the Royal Academy for its exhibition in 1862. [20]

Whistler and Jo decided that they wanted to go to Spain and stopped on the way on the southwestern coast of France in the Basque country. Whistler painted a number of powerful seascapes there. However, in a letter to Fantin-Latour, he wrote: "I admit you are right. 'Plein-air' painting should be done at home. [...]

15. See page 19.

16. Wapping and Rotherhithe were a maze of narrow streets along the Thames and were considered among the most squalid areas in London.

17. See page 23.

18. Musée du Louvre, Paris.

19. David Park Curry. *James McNeill Whistler at the Freer Gallery of Art.* New York, London: W.W. Norton & Co, 1984, p. 38.

20. The painting was exhibited at a gallery in Berners Street, London.

Blue and Silver
Blue Wave. Biarritz, 1862
Oil on canvas
65.8 × 90 cm
(25 ½" × 35 ¼")
Hill-Stead Museum
Farmington, Connecticut

Something is there for one minute and then gone for good. You put down the true and pure tone, you catch it in flight as you kill a bird in the air — and then the public demands a polished picture." Ever a nomad, Whistler moved in March 1863 to a house in Chelsea, at 7 Lindsey Row, near old Battersea Bridge. In April he traveled to Holland with Legros to study Rembrandt's etchings. His own etchings won him a gold medal at an exhibition in The Hague. During that journey he stopped off in Paris to see his friends, but he was very much a Londoner now. He was close to the Pre-Raphaelites, Rossetti, Edward Burne-Jones, William Morris, and the poet Algernon Swinburne, whom he introduced to Manet. Whistler was a conspicuous figure in clubs and drawing rooms, cultivated the ladies, and became the envy of other socialites by collecting Chinese porcelain and Japanese prints. He was also becoming famous for his extravagant clothes, his verbal sallies and practical jokes, and his eclectic taste.

A SCANDAL, THEN FAME

The White Girl was rejected by the Salon of 1863, as was Manet's *Picnic*. This was not the first time that the jury's decision had reflected such hostility toward avant-garde painting, but that year an exceptionally large number of pictures were left out of the exhibition and the artists were furious. The uproar was such that Napoleon III decided that the rejected entries should be exhibited separately. Seven hundred and eighty-one canvases were shown at the Salon des Refusés.

Manet and Whistler were singled out for derision by the public. The reasons given were the same in both cases: Their paintings were slapdash, the theme "vulgar", the draftsmanship mediocre, there was no attempt to maintain the subordination of components, and color was used to emphasize volumes rather than outline shapes. *The White Lady* (as it was called in the catalogue) was particularly badly received. It was hung near one of the entrances so as to make it impossible to miss. In his book, "L'Œuvre", Emile Zola tells how before this "very curious vision seen through the eye of a great artist, people were nudging each other, doubling up with laughter, and there was always a group standing about with open-mouthed hilarity." Together with *The Picnic*, Whistler's entry was the greatest joke at the exhibition, and it was greeted with disgust and horror by many. One exception, according to a letter Fantin-Latour wrote to Whistler in Amsterdam at the time, was Baudelaire, who "finds it charming, totally exquisite". He added, "Legros, Manet, Bracquemond, and myself, we all think it admirable". He reported that Courbet called his picture "an apparition" but that he liked it. The critic Fernand Desnoyers, in his "Salon des Refusés: La Peinture en 1863", agreed with Courbet that Whistler's *White Girl* was "the portrait of a spirit, a medium". Jules Antoine Castagnary saw in it the depiction of a young woman on the morning after her bridal night, "that troubling moment when [she] reflects on the absence of yesterday's virginity."[21] Critics used the words "apparition" and "vision", and Jo found herself credited with the "vacant stare of Ophelia". Théophile Thoré-Bürger found "an indefinable trace of Goya and even Velázquez in the portrayal of the woman." Paul Mantz and Ernest Chesneau were disconcerted by Manet's *Picnic* (Mantz thought the painting "unsound"), but they liked Whistler's entry. Chesneau praised what he called "a romantic imagination of dream and poetry".[22] Whistler could have replied as he had done to a London critic: "My painting merely shows a girl dressed in white standing in front of a white curtain."

The White Girl is regarded by many as a sort of contrived revival of dreamy Romanticism, or as a transition from Naturalism to Symbolism, but above all as a splendid pictorial achievement which deserves admiration. There begins Whistler's subjective approach to nature, a sort of hallucinatory aestheticism which was to delight writers and poets. Whistler's reality was always closer to dreams than to life.

He became increasingly close to Rossetti, whom he had met in July 1862. Rossetti was one of the few friends with whom he did not later fall out. It is true that Rossetti regarded him as an important innovator in painting — as indeed did a number of his Pre-Raphaelite friends. Whistler invited Rossetti to join him in a group exhibition with Legros and Fantin-Latour, whose *Homage to Delacroix* was well received at the Salon of 1864. Fantin-Latour was, with Legros, a member of Whistler's newly formed "Société des Trois", and Whistler was delighted by Fantin-Latour's success, though he was disappointed that Rossetti had not been included in the painting. At the same time, and quite probably at Rossetti's instigation, Whistler replaced his signature with his famous butterfly motif, which not only contained his initial but stood as a symbol of his restless to-ing and fro-ing in life.

21. Jules Antoine Castagnary. *Salons (1857- 1879)*. Paris, 1892, I, pp. 179. Quoted in David Curry, *op. cit.*, p. 41.

22. Paul Mantz. "Salon de 1863" in *Gazette des Beaux-Arts* 15 (1863): pp. 60-61. Ernest Chesneau. *L'Art et les artistes modernes*. Paris, 1864. Quoted in David Curry, *op. cit.*, pp. 39-40.

Symphony in White No. 1
The White Girl, 1862
Oil on canvas
214.7 × 108 cm
(84½" × 42½")
National Gallery of Art
Washington, D.C.
Harris Whittemore
Collection

At this early stage, the Japanese influence which could be detected in his work was limited to the use of Oriental accessories. Later Whistler assimilated Japanese principles of color and design. In *Caprice in Purple and Gold: The Golden Screen*[23] and *Purple and Rose: The Lange Leizen of the Six Marks*,[24] both from 1864, Jo poses in a kimono surrounded by the Oriental decor of the studio. The latter painting seems to have caused Whistler considerable difficulty and he wrote to Fantin-Latour: "It represents a porcelain dealer, a Chinese woman painting pottery. But it is difficult and I am having to scrape so much off and start again!

23. See page 26.

24. The Philadelphia Museum of Art. The title evokes the Delft name for 18th-century, blue and white, Chinese porcelain decorated with figures and the potter's marks on the bottom of the vases.

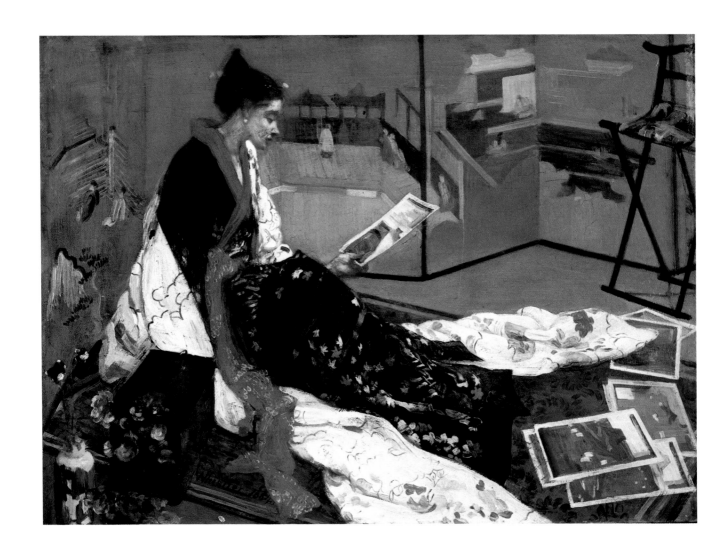

Caprice No. 2 in Purple
and Gold: The Golden
Screen, 1864
Oil on panel
50.2 × 68.7 cm (19¾" × 27")
The Freer Gallery of Art
Smithsonian Institution
Washington, D.C.

The Artist in His Studio
Ca 1864
Oil on panel
62.5 × 47.4 cm
(24¾" × 18¾")
The Art Institute, Chicago
Friends of American Art
Collection

There are times when I think I have learned something, and then I am deeply discouraged." There was nothing to worry about! When *Wapping on Thames* was exhibited at the Royal Academy in 1864, the London "Times" critic paid him an overwhelming compliment and compared his style to Velázquez's. The following year a similar reception greeted *The Little White Girl*, which was also given the title of *Symphony in White No. 2.*[25] It was the theme of Swinburne's poem "Before the Mirror", two lines of which were inscribed on the frame by Whistler:

25. See page 25.

> My hand, a fallen rose
> Lies snow-white on white snow, and take no care.

La Princesse du Pays de la Porcelaine was feted at the Salon of 1865. In it a heroine stands, as Thoré-Bürger wrote, "luminous like those women the imagination appears to descry in the clouds" in the willowy attitude of an Oriental woman, but her posture has the anachronistic charm of a Pre-Raphaelite virgin. The composition also displays Japanese effects in the large, asymmetrical planes of the screen and the carpet. The overall impression is of a simplicity of presentation and an economy in the distribution of colors, in which cheap exoticism is largely eschewed. At the time, Japonisme was at the height of fashion in both Paris and London, following a general enthusiasm created by the Second World Fair in London in 1862.

The sketch for *The Balcony* is much freer in style and more subdued in color — gray, faded rose and green —[26] than the finished painting, which is also entitled *Variations in Flesh Color and Green*.[27] Begun in 1864 — but Whistler continued to work on it over the next six years — it is a work typical of his early japonesque style. It depicts young women in kimonos on the artist's balcony overlooking the Thames. Whistler shows a lack of ease in his handling of the figures in space and open daylight — the composition is rather conventional. However, the unexpected combination of a Japanese scene in the foreground and a background of factories and smokestacks on the other side of the Thames gives the painting a certain drama.

26. 1867-1870, Hunterian Art Gallery, University of Glasgow.

27. See page 38.

28. See page 30.

WHY DID I NOT STUDY UNDER INGRES?

In the fall of 1865, Whistler and Jo were in Trouville, where Courbet was painting "nature in its nature" at this fashionable waterside resort populated by aristocratic idlers and wide-eyed elegant women. Courbet was quite taken by the beautiful Irishwoman. Whistler and Courbet painted together. The latter wrote complacently to his father, on November 17, "The painter Whistler is here with me — an Englishman [sic] who is my pupil." He also painted two portraits of Jo.

The wide expanse of the North Sea, with its gray skies and subtle plays of light and shadow, was a new source of inspiration for Whistler. His seascapes are done in broad horizontal brushstrokes. They are quite different from the Impressionist paintings which were to come, but they anticipate Impressionism through their broad perspective and the importance given to light without any anecdote or embellishment. Degas admired them, and they are, to borrow Degas's phrase used in speaking of his own work, "states of the eyes". Whistler made a series of outstanding seascapes, one of which, *Harmony in Blue and Silver. Trouville*,[28] shows a small figure in the foreground who is almost certainly Courbet, standing on the shore gazing out to sea, just

Rose and Silver
"La Princesse du Pays de
la Porcelaine", 1863-1864
Oil on canvas
199.9 × 116.1 cm
(78¾" × 45¾")
The Freer Gallery of Art
Smithsonian Institution
Washington, D.C.

as Courbet had depicted himself in 1854 saluting the Mediterranean.[29]   With *The Wave*,[30] *Trouville*,[31] and *Sea and Rain*, it ranks among the most impressive and sensitive impressions of that almost wintry encounter between Whistler and the open sea.   Courbet's influence is especially noticeable in the sweeping brushstokes, the sense of movement, and the synthetic grasp of space.   This was already discernible in two beautiful landscapes painted a year before, *Chelsea in Ice* and *Battersea Reach from Lindsey Houses*,[32] in which an Oriental inspiration is revealed by a barely suggested distance and by subtle effects of colorless, atmospheric perspective due to harmonies of neutral tones.   Three japonesque figures are placed in the foreground of the Battersea picture, giving scale to a landscape in which water is shrouded in mist.   The seascapes are the most eloquent and successful examples of Courbet's influence.   It was enhanced by Whistler's taste for effects of light, swelling waves, and turbulent skies, a taste shared at the time by Pissarro, Renoir, and especially Monet.   Among the lessons they learned from Courbet was the preparation of the canvas in brown (except that Monet preferred to paint directly on a white canvas), which brought out the play of colored masses.   They were also inspired by Courbet's swaying rhythms — his broad technique which had so impressed Eugène Boudin when painting with Courbet at Le Havre — his confident and vigorous brushwork, and his remarkable faith in his own accurate vision and bold painting.

Harmony in Blue and Silver: Trouville, 1865
Oil on canvas
50 × 76 cm
(19 $^{11}/_{16}$" × 29 $^{15}/_{16}$")
Isabelle Stewart Gardner Museum, Boston

29. *The Seaside at Palavas*, Musée Fabre, Montpellier.

30. Montclair Art Museum, Montclair, New Jersey.

31. The Art Institute, Chicago.

32. Hunterian Art Gallery, University of Glasgow.

Sea and Rain, 1865
Oil on canvas
50.7 × 72.6 cm
(20" × 28½")
Museum of Art, University
of Michigan, Ann Arbor
Bequest of M.W. Parker

The Ocean, 1866
Oil on canvas
80.7 × 101.9 cm
(31¾" × 40⅛")
The Frick Collection
New York

Whistler was always inspired by the sea, ports, boats, and rivers — the symbols of nomadism and the "other places" celebrated by Baudelaire. As soon as he settled in London, he chose to live in Chelsea, because he was irresistibly drawn to the working-class life of the docks and the narrow streets leading down to the Thames. However, he did not conceal his mistrust of nature. For Whistler, a landscape was only an impression and, unlike Courbet and the Impressionists, he never attached a great importance to the nature he depicted. He believed that nature should not be labored but should mainly provide background and fleeting effects, and that it was enough to show virtuosity and a sense of poetry to be in the same league as Monet or Renoir. While the Impressionists took such pains to study light directly from nature, Whistler was merely interested in the effects produced by that light — mist, rain, veiled sunrays, *Arrangements*, *Symphonies*, *Harmonies*, and *Variations*. This may be the weakness of his work, as it is with Fantin-Latour, who limited himself to a joyless, almost suffocating, intimist style, devoid of any flight of imagination or freedom. Despite this movement away from Realism, Whistler never turned his back on nature and, indeed, his behavior and pronouncements upon "plein-air" painting remained full of contradictions.

On January 31, 1866, he sailed for South America with his brother William and several refugees from the Confederate Army. They arrived in the Chilean port of Valparaiso, on March 12, and they witnessed the bombardment of the town by the Spanish fleet. One may wonder why he embarked upon this journey. Was it a sudden quest for adventure and heroic deeds, or was it really to support the valiant people of Peru and their Chilean allies against the Spaniards? It remains a mystery, and it is difficult to picture this Chelsea dandy as a Byronic hero. Jo may have had something to do with his expedition. Not only did she pose for Courbet, but she had also become his mistress. As a consequence, Whistler developed a violent aversion to Courbet personally and he also rejected his influence as a painter. *Twilight in Flesh Color and Green*, a painting shimmering with the ships' reflections in the water, is one of the views of Valparaiso harbor which illustrate this departure from Courbet's realism.[33]

33. Tate Gallery, London.

Whistler was back in London in October and immediately broke off with Jo. In February 1867 he moved to 2 Lindsey Row (now 36 Cheyne Walk), where he was to live until 1878. He exhibited three paintings at the Royal Academy. In April he went to Paris, where he may have seen Ingres's retrospective exhibition. In May he wrote a letter to Fantin-Latour that documents the violence of the crisis he was going through. It is an extraordinary letter: "The time of my arrival [in Paris] was very bad for me. Courbet — his influence — has been disgusting [sic]. The regret that I feel, and the rage and even hatred that I have toward all that might surprise you, but this is the explanation. It is neither poor Courbet nor his work that I reject. [...] I still recognize his qualities." But what he rejected was the notion that "one had only to open one's eyes and paint whatever one found in front of one! Beautiful nature and the whole caboodle!" Repudiating Courbet's influence, "because I am very individual and because I was rich in qualities which he never had and which suited me," he added: "It is just that this damn realism appealed at once to my painter's vanity! And mocking all traditions, it cried at the top of its lungs, with confident ignorance, 'Long live nature!' Nature! My dear, this cry caused me great misfortune." In the same letter, he continued: "Oh my friend! Why did I not study under Ingres? I do not say that purely as a rhapsody [sic] in front of his paintings. I like them very little. [...] It is true, color is life. [...] Held securely on leash by a master draftsman, color is a glorious creature [...] but

Nocturne in Blue and Gold
Valparaiso Bay, 1866
Oil on canvas
95.5 × 70.8 cm
(37 ⅝" × 27 ⅞")
The Freer Gallery of Art
Smithsonian Institution
Washington, D.C.

Symphony in White No. 3
1865-1867
Oil on canvas
51.1 × 76.8 cm
(20 ¼" × 30 ⅛")
The Barber Institute
of Fine Arts
University of Birmingham

coupled with uncertainty [...] color becomes a saucy whore wasting its talent on whatever it likes and not takings things seriously as long as it finds them charming. [...] You can see the result! Chaotic intoxication, deceit, regrets." The reference to Ingres served as a counterweight to Courbet's "disgusting" influence. It seems, however, that Whistler did not fully understand the role nature and color played in avant-garde painting. By turning his back upon them he was finding his own path, a "closed" Realism as opposed to the "open" Realism of the Impressionists. He did not deny the beauty of nature but placed more emphasis on its decorative aspect, to which he devoted his virtuosity and his taste.

The artistic and personal crisis which Whistler was undergoing at the time separated him from all the friends of his early years except Fantin-Latour. His character also changed. He became the worldly, vain, somewhat shrill aesthete with bizarre mannerisms and a shady reputation whose image has come down to posterity. He even came to blows with his brother-in-law, Seymour Haden — it is said that it happened at the Paris World Fair of 1867, after the sudden death of James Reeves Traer who was Haden's associate and Whistler's friend.

Variations in Blue and Green, ca 1868
Oil on millboard mounted on wood panel, 46.9 × 61.8 cm (18½" × 24¾")
The Freer Gallery of Art Smithsonian Institution Washington, D.C.

34. Addison Gallery of American Art, Andover, Massachusetts.

The World Fair was the occasion of Whistler's major success in France. He exhibited several paintings in the American pavilion — *Brown and Silver: Old Battersea Bridge,*[34] *Wapping on Thames, The White Girl, Twilight in Flesh Color*

Rose and Gray
Three Figures
1868-1878
Oil on canvas
139.1 × 185.4 cm
(54¾" × 73")
The Tate Gallery, London

and Green: Valparaiso — alongside some etchings. The reviews were favorable, but either because he did not consider them sufficient praise or for some other reason, Whistler did not exhibit his work again at the Salon for fifteen years.

NOCTURNES AND PORTRAITS

Then came a period of restless experimentation, of *Arrangements* and *Variations*, which gave expression to Whistler uncertainties but also to his desire for an art he held to be more elevated and complete than Realism. He discovered the art of Albert Moore, whose classically draped studies of women were based on Tanagra figurines, and temporarily abandoned his combination of japonesque

Variations in Flesh Color
and Green: The Balcony, 186/
Oil on panel
61.4 × 48.8 cm（24¼" × 14¼)
The Freer Gallery of Art
Smithsonian Institution
Washington, D.C.

Nocturne in Blue and
Silver
1872-1873
Oil on canvas
44.4 × 61 cm (17½" × 24")
Private Collection
U.S.A.

Chelsea Bridge and Church
1870-1871
Drypoint, VI/VI
10.2 × 16.7 cm (4" × 6 9/16")
The Freer Gallery of Art
Smithsonian Institution
Washington, D.C.

composition and Pre-Raphaelite figures for a style giving pride of place to line. *Three Figures: Pink and Gray* is an example of this style, a somewhat weak composition to which the study entitled *Symphony in White: Three Girls* may be preferred for its freer handling and rich paints.[35] He failed to complete the *Six Projects*,[36] and did not produce anything for public view in 1868 or 1869. In 1870 he exhibited *The Balcony* at the Royal Academy, and the following year saw the publication of the *Thames Set*. He also began a series of *Nocturnes* inspired by the Thames (first entitled *Clair de Lune*), which display delicate effects of veiled light together with glimpses of landscape half-hidden by mist — chimneystacks, bridges, ships, flashing lights.

In 1864 Whistler was introduced by Rossetti to a Liverpool shipping magnate, Frederick Richards Leyland, who bought some of his paintings and etchings, gave him large advances, and provided him with important commissions for the next thirteen years. Whistler often stayed at Speke Hall, Leyland's country estate near Liverpool, or at his large town house at Prince's Gate in London. Whistler painted portraits of his hosts, starting with lively sketches, and then making more conventional pictures, such as *Arrangement in Black: Portrait of F. R. Leyland* in 1870-1873, a *Symphony in Flesh Color and Rose* for his wife in 1871-1874,[37] and portraits of their daughters, on which he worked for just as long. Between 1870 and 1875 he made eighteen etchings and drypoints of members of the Leyland family and subjects taken from Speke Hall.

In 1870 the Franco-Prussian broke out, followed by the revolutionary Commune in Paris. Monet and Pissarro found asylum in London. Pissarro recalled that they were "especially struck by [English] landscape artists, who were more in agreement with our views on 'open-air' painting, light and fleeting effects: Watts, Rossetti, among the Moderns", but it seems that they had little to do with Whistler. Nevertheless, Whistler got to know the dealer Paul Durand-Ruel. He showed his work at his gallery at 168 New Bond Street, where the young and courageous dealer exhibited paintings by the future Impressionists and by Camille Corot, Jean-François Millet, Théodore Rousseau, and Courbet.

35. The Freer Gallery of Art, Washington, D.C.

36. A group of oil sketches for a never-completed scheme of architectural decoration. The Freer Gallery of Art, Washington, D.C.

37. The Frick Collection, New York.

Arrangement in Black
Portrait of F.R. Leyland
1870-1873
Oil on canvas
192.8 × 91.9 cm
(75 7/8" × 36 1/8")
The Freer Gallery of Art
Smithsonian Institution
Washington, D.C.

The Silk Dress, 1873
Drypoint, I/II
20.8 × 13.2 cm
(8 3⁄16" × 5 3⁄16")
The Freer Gallery of Art
Smithsonian Institution
Washington, D.C.

The Velvet Dress, 1873
Drypoint, I/V
23.2 × 15.8 cm
(9⅛" × 6⅜")
The Freer Gallery of Art
Smithsonian Institution
Washington, D.C.

Speke Hall, 1870
Etching and
drypoint, II/IX
22.5 × 15 cm
(8⅞" × 5⅞")
The Freer Gallery of Art
Smithsonian Institution
Washington, D.C.

Nocturne in Blue and Gold
Old Battersea Bridge
1872-1875
Oil on canvas
68.3 × 51.2 cm
(26⅞" × 20⅛")
The Tate Gallery, London

The *Nocturnes* were based more on visual memory than on the direct observation of nature, and the color harmonies were of more interest to Whistler for their effect than for their truth. This drew him away from the preoccupations out of which Impressionism was to arise, but it brought him closer to what was to become the Symbolist movement. J.-K. Huysmans was to describe his paintings as "dream landscapes". Whistler painted one of his most japonesque *Nocturnes* — *Blue and Gold: Old Battersea Bridge.* The bridge stands out as a gigantic

Arrangement in Gray and
Black No. 1. Portrait of
the Painter's Mother, 1871
Oil on canvas
144.3 × 162.5 cm
(56¾" × 64")
Musée d'Orsay, Paris
Photo Réunion des
Musées Nationaux, Paris

Arrangement in Gray and
Black No. 2. Portrait of
Thomas Carlyle
1872-1873
Oil on canvas
171.1 × 143.5 cm
(67¼" × 56½")
Glasgow Art Gallery
and Museum

ghostly silhouette in dark blue against the soft blue-green tinges of the water and sky, with pale flashes of light briefly illuminating the mysterious darkness. He also painted views of Cremorne Gardens, in which the fleeting impressions of nocturnal scenes, the faint lights, and the unreal looking figures contribute to an atmosphere out of Paul Verlaine's poems or Watteau's paintings.

Whistler's portraits at that time were "ideal constructions", which re-created the inner nature of their subjects against a carefully composed setting while also capturing the essence of their appearance, psychology, and social position. His painting of his mother, dating from 1871, and that of Thomas Carlyle, from 1872-1873, both entitled *Arrangement in Gray and Black,* are fine examples from this period.[38] Both are works of great strength; both are austere and show a remarkable economy of means, in particular a restricted use of color. *The Portrait of the Painter's Mother* was initially rejected by the Royal Academy and then accepted with reservation — one possible explanation of why Whistler never again exhibited his work there — and it was far from bring unanimously applauded by the British public, which — through exposure to the Pre-Raphaelites and the eclectics — had been accustomed to paintings illustrating a moral theme and exemplifying a tradition that was both humanistic and aesthetic. By replacing representational painting with a musical concept of an arrangement or harmony, Whistler was breaking with Naturalism and an art as restful and comforting to the eye as to the mind. His art resided in mystery, in the power of suggestion, and in the aura surrounding silent subjects. It could only provoke mixed feelings or outright hostility. The colors seemed unreal, the composition staged, the subject matter arbitrary. The essentially aristocratic order of things to which Whistler aspired by means of a style of painting expressing pure sensation was largely lost on his contemporaries, who saw in his work little but the effusion of a dandy. In both Paris and London, Whistler was subjected to violent attacks. "Other artists and a few connoisseurs admired his work," wrote Durand-Ruel in his memoirs, "but his paintings were too fine and on too lofty a plane to be understood [...] and I never succeeded in selling any."[39]

The Portrait of the Painter's Mother represents a landmark in Whistler's development. The work establishes that painting as an art exists for its own sake. The picture is a self-sufficient reality, which draws its essence from harmonies of tones, nuances, values, its contrasts of colors, and from the hidden resonance of things. This was too much for the British public. Only when the French National Collection bought the portrait in 1891 did attitudes toward Whistler soften in British artistic circles, culminating in a final, albeit, belated triumph. Nevertheless, true connoisseurs were able to appreciate this work from the start. Rossetti declared that the painting "should make one happy for life". The Leylands hung it next to a Velázquez and assured that it stood up to comparison. It was exhibited at the Salon in 1883, to mixed reviews. The "Univers Illustré" disliked the mournful scene of "an old lady abandoned in a room with a smoking grate," but "Le Rappel" praised the delicacy of the picture and its subtle touches in grays, while Charles Bigot, in the "Gazette des Beaux-Arts", admired the "harmony between the color and the subject."

His portrait of Miss Cicely Alexander, *Harmony in Gray and Green,* completes the trilogy begun with the artist's mother and Thomas Carlyle. This was the first of a series of portraits of six daughters of William Alexander, a banker. Of the portraits of the other sisters, only that of Agnes-Mary — nicknamed May — at the Tate Gallery and that of Florence, at the Portland Museum of Art in Maine, have

38. See pages 46 and 47.

39. Lionello Venturi. *Les Archives de l'Impressionnisme.* Paris, New York, 1939.

Harmony in Gray and Green
Miss Cicely Alexander
1872-1874
Oil on canvas
190 × 98.7 cm
(74⅞" × 38½")
The Tate Gallery, London

Arrangement in Yellow
and Gray
Effie Deans
1876
Oil on canvas
194 × 93 cm
(76 ⅜" × 36 ⅝")
Rijksmuseum
Amsterdam

Nocturne in Gray and Gold
Chelsea Snow, 1876
Oil on canvas
47.2 × 65.5 cm
(18 ⅝" × 24 ⅝")
Fogg Art Museum, Harvard
University, Cambridge
Massachusetts. Bequest of
Grenville L. Winthrop

Portrait of
Miss Rosa Corder
1875-1878
Oil on canvas
192.4 × 92.4 cm
(75 ¾" × 36 ⅜")
The Frick Collection
New York

Arrangement in White
and Black, ca 1876
Oil on canvas
191.4 × 90.9 cm
(75⅜" × 35¾")
The Freer Gallery of Art
Smithsonian Institution
Washington, D.C.

survived. The portrait of Cicely took seventy sittings. It does not have the austerity or the sadness which fitted the elderly models of the two other portraits, but it is not exactly cheerful either. The young girl looks very earnest or even sullen. The different shades of grays — iron gray, greenish gray, ivory gray — and blacks are subtly harmonized. The sad-eyed infantas of Velázquez are not far away.

Whistler held his first one-man show in June 1874 at the Flemish Gallery in London: thirteen paintings, thirty-six drawings, and fifty etchings were exhibited in a fashionable setting of ornamental plants, flowers, and blue and white porcelain. The show was well received, but the artist was praised more for his elegance than for his talent. The following year he exhibited several *Nocturnes*, which were largely misunderstood and even ridiculed. He took it badly, and he made the matters worse by provoking Leyland's rage and by launching a libel suit against John Ruskin.

The story goes that when he went away on one of his trips, Mr. Leyland gave him the keys to his town house in Prince's Gate with instructions to restore the Cordoba leather panels in the dining room, which already housed *La Princesse du Pays de la Porcelaine*. The painter held court in his host's absence and he transformed he interior into a mock Buddhist temple, which became the *Peacock Room*.[40] The leather was permanently altered, and Leyland angrily refused to pay for a design which he had not commissioned. Whistler had given rein to all the decorative fads of an entire period, and the room sums up the aesthetic demands of a sophisticated coterie who thought that beauty must be intricate and unusual. The *Princesse* was set in a glittering scene of blue and gold, with large stylized birds anticipating Art Nouveau designs. It enchanted Whistler and he went about trying to win over his detractors with what can only be called a public relations campaign. However, Leyland's anger — more at the insolent way in which Whistler had behaved than at the work itself, which he kept — turned public opinion partly against the artist. Insults, claims for money, and threats were traded in correspondence, and there was almost a duel. It was the first time Whistler's flattering, though controversial, reputation had been dented.

In May 1877, Whistler contributed eight paintings, including *Nocturnes*, for the opening of the Grosvenor Gallery. They were shown side by side with works by Millais, Alma-Tadema, Burne-Jones, Leighton, and Poynter, the leading lights of English Victorian painting — every one of which had been the butt of his rudeness at one time or another! Ruskin, the famous art critic, exploded when he saw the asking price for *Nocturne in Black and Gold: The Falling Rocket*, one of Whistler's most spectacular use of light and one of his most freely handled. One may wonder whether the violent rage it provoked in the irascible critic was justified by Whistler's constant impertinence, or whether there were other reasons. In Letter 79 of the monthly "Fors Clavigera", which appeared on July 2, Ruskin declared that the proprietor of the gallery, Sir Coutts Lindsey, "ought not to have admitted works into the gallery in which the ill educated conceit of the artist so nearly approached the aspect of willful imposture. I have seen, and heard, much of cockney impudence before now; but never expected to hear a coxcomb ask two hundred guineas for flinging a pot of paint in the public's face." Following this stinging attack, Whistler was unable to sell his paintings. Although he first tried to ignore Ruskin's comments, he was faced with mounting debts. He sued Ruskin for libel and thereby turned the exhibition into a public scandal. Crowds flocked to the exhibition, taking sides either for the critic or the artist. The newspapers took up the story, and

40. After Leyland's death in 1892, his house was sold and the *Peacock Room* underwent several changes in ownership. It was acquired by C.L. Freer, who had it dismantled and moved to his house in Detroit, where it was reassembled. He bequeathed it to the Freer Gallery of Art in Washington, D.C., where, after restoration in 1947-1949, it now stands.

Nocturne in Black and Gold
The Falling Rocket
Ca 1874
Oil on panel
60.3 × 46.7 cm
(23¾" × 18⅜")
The Detroit Institute
of Arts. Gift of
Dexter M. Ferry Jr.

The Peacock Room
Harmony in Blue and Gold
(North-East Corner)
1876-1877
Oil paints and gold
on leather and wood
4.26 × 10.11 × 6.08 m
(13'9⅞" × 33'2" × 19'11½")
The Freer Gallery of Art
Smithsonian Institution
Washington, D.C.

Whistler decided to take advantage of the stir caused by the offending article and by reports in "Punch" and "The Times" (which wrote that Whistler had earned a place among the characters of his day) and sought to add the halo of a martyr to his reputation for insolence. The trial to determine a painting's quality, its proper price, and the independence of a critic, must have been one of the most improbable disputes ever to have come before a court. The attorney general compounded the ridiculousness of the whole affair when he bewailed the fact that certain people nourished a liking for the incomprehensible and he stated that the admiration for *Harmonies, Nocturnes, Symphonies,* and *Arrangements* was not a craze to be encouraged and that Ruskin was entitled to say so.

Although the final verdict was in Whistler's favor, after some fairly hilarious scenes in court, he was awarded contemptuous damages of one farthing and he was saddled with the enormous costs of the action. Furthermore he had not sold a painting in two years, his debts after the Leyland fracas had only mounted higher, he had been building a mansion at great expense — the "White House" — and sales of his Japanese prints and other possessions did not realize enough. In May 1879 he was declared bankrupt, with Leyland as his chief creditor.

Nocturne
1879-1880
Etching and drypoint, IV/V
20 × 29.5 cm
(7¼" × 11⅝")
National Gallery of Art
Washington, D.C.
Rosenwald Collection

Nocturne in Blue and Gold
The Lagoon, Venice
1879-1880
Oil on canvas
50.8 × 65.4 cm (20" × 25¾")
Museum of Fine Arts
Boston
Emily L. Ainsley Fund

Nocturne: Palaces
1879-1880
Etching and drypoint
on laid paper, VII/IX
29.6 × 20.1 cm
(11 ⅝" × 7 ⅞")
The Art Gallery of
Ontario, Toronto. Gift of
Esther and Arthur Gelber

He was very lucky to receive a commission from the Fine Art Society for a set of etchings of Venice.   He left London at the beginning of September accompanied by his then model and mistress, Maud Franklin, and spent a year in Venice.

Two Doorways
1880
Etching and
drypoint, VI/VI
20 × 29.1 cm
(8" × 11½")
National Gallery of Art
Washington, D.C.
Rosenwald Collection

The Palaces, 1880
Etching and
drypoint, II/III
24.9 × 35.8 cm
(9¾" × 14 1/16")
National Gallery of Art
Washington, D.C.
Gift of Mr. and
Mrs. J. Watson Webb

The Rialto, 1880
Etching and
drypoint, II/II
29.3 × 20 cm
(11½" × 7⅞")
National Gallery of Art
Washington, D.C.
Gift of Mr. and
Mrs. J. Watson Webb

MARVELOUS "SETS" ON VENICE

There he painted delicate pastels consisting of *Arrangements* in which an enclosed view of a canal, a trattoria with a faded front, a palazzo doorway, or the side of a shop was enough for him to weave his virtuoso skill about an unusual color harmony.   Often, however, he did not rise above that, remaining content to be an appreciative lounger taking down a tone here or a chord there.   He set to work

Garden, 1880
Etching and
and drypoint, IV/VIII
30 × 23.8 cm (12" × 9¼")
The Metropolitan Museum
of Art, New York
Harris Brisbane Dick Fund

on the etchings and, between September and December, he produced sixteen plates. Unlike his pastels, his Venetian etchings had only limited success. In 1880 there was a first London exhibition, comprising a set of twelve, followed by a second in 1883, which showed fifty-one pieces, largely dominated by Venice and published three years later.

He then turned his attention to street scenes in London, in a series of small, lively plates that are close in their handling of light and air to contemporary French Impressionist etchings. A handful of these prints were included in the 1883 exhibition. In 1886 he held his second one-man show, entitled *Notes, Harmonies, Nocturnes*. The following year he made another visit to Holland and Belgium, published six lithographs, *Art Notes*, and etched twelve plates while attending the Naval Review marking Queen Victoria's Golden Jubilee.

Venetian Court, 1879
Drypoint, II/III
29.1 × 20 cm
(11 ½" × 7 ⅞")
The Freer Gallery of Art
Smithsonian Institution
Washington, D.C.

Now that it is possible that it is possible to clear away some of the extravagance of personality which dominated contemporaries' view of the painter, we discover that he was a remarkable engraver. He was one of the first to work the plates directly from nature, and his landscapes, particularly of Venice,

have an admirable clarity and firmness. The artist's vision was captivated less by the theme, the landscape, than by tone values and sonorities suggesting the essentials of the scene in a few strokes, or hatchings, sometimes incorporating brilliantly inventive flourishes, refusing the merely picturesque. These views, in which Venice was more imagined than analyzed, though seen with an astonishingly perceptive eye, were not understood. They were considered unfinished. However, they show a painter's eye, which uses black and gray, particularly in the second set, to add a vaporous softness to the shimmering forms, thereby introducing an element of aerial perspective in which space seems to be suspended in the half-light between sky and water. Whistler was not an artist of broad daylight. At a time when the Impressionists were recording dazzling sunlight, he opted for shadows, dusk, and night time, though he shared their attachment to fleeting effects that signify the irretrievable moments of life. His approach was to bite the metal lightly, proceeding by suggestions rather than blatant emphasis. In his etchings, just as in his paintings, the overwhelming impression is one of repose, in which subtle gradations of tone are expressed with the utmost economy and the scene implies intimacy or silence. He treated his sitters with extraordinary delicacy and showed a similar restraint and fervent

Old Putney Bridge, 1879
Etching and
drypoint, IV/V
20.1 × 29.5 cm
(7 15/16" × 11 5/8")
National Gallery of Art
Washington, D.C.
Rosenwald Collection

The "Adam and Eve"
Old Chelsea, 1879
Etching and
drypoint, II/II
17.3 × 30.2 cm
(6 7/8" × 11 7/8")
The Art Gallery of Ontario
Toronto. Gift of Inco Ltd.

observation in his landscapes.   Whether he was using the etcher's needle or the paintbrush, he maintained a constant lightness of touch, starting from the surface of things to yield their inner essence.

This artistic subtlety is in stark contrast to Whistler's character in life, which became even wittier, sharper, and more unpredictable after the trial. Unfortunately he had the worst friends that could be wished on him at the time — his entourage included Oscar Wilde, whose own extravagant and exhibitionist behavior encouraged worse from him, not to speak of the accusations of immorality that the friendship provoked in others.

41. *Arrangement in Black, Lady Meux*, Honolulu Academy of Arts, Hawaii; *Harmony in Rose and Gray: Portrait of Lady Meux*, see page 68; *Portrait of Lady Meux With Her Furs*, is no longer extant.

Luckily, Whistler met Valerie, Lady Meux, the wife of a rich brewer, very much a member of the fashionable circles of the time, who commissioned a portrait.   He painted three portraits of her between 1881 and 1886.[41]   They do not have the distinction of earlier portraits, although the first, exhibited at the Salon of 1882, impressed Degas, who found it "very striking, and refined to the point of excess, but what spirit!" As so often happened with him, Whistler managed to offend his model, and the third portrait remained unfinished.

Whistler returned to favor with the public, and dashed off one portrait after another, commissioned or otherwise.   They are perceptive, sophisticated, and subtle portraits, often painted with a quick brush, with constant experiments of composition and colors.   Some reach the limits of visual pyrotechnics, such as *Arrangement in Flesh Color and Black: Portrait of Théodore Duret*,[42] which shows

42. See page 69.

Harmony in Pink
and Gray
Portrait of Lady Meux
1881-1882
Oil on canvas
193.7 × 93.5 cm
(76 ¼" × 36 ⅝")
The Frick Collection
New York

Arrangement in Flesh Color
and Black. Portrait of
Théodore Duret, 1883-1884
Oil on canvas
193.2 × 90.8 cm
(76⅛" × 35¾")
The Metropolitan Museum
of Art, New York
C.L. Wolfe Collection

The Village Sweet-Shop
1884-1886
Etching, I/I
8.5 × 12.4 cm
(3¼" × 4⅞")
The Freer Gallery of Art
Smithsonian Institution
Washington, D.C.

the critic in black evening dress with a pink domino cape against an arm and holding a fan. These accessories caused a stir at the time, but the picture is above all a set of successful color contrasts, in spite of the severity of the jacket and the plain background.

Oscar Wilde appointed himself as Whistler's impresario. He praised his work in a series of lectures given in the United States. Of his etchings, Lucien Pissarro wrote to his father, "He does wonderful things with a few lines." Pissarro wrote back, "The suppleness you find in them, the pithiness and delicacy which charm you derive from the inking which is done by Whistler himself; no professional printer could substitute for him, for inking is an art in itself and complete the etched line."[43] This was the tribute of one craftsman to another, though it did not prevent him from also saying that Whistler could be a bit of a fraud at times.

43. Quoted in John Rewald, *Camille Pissarro: Letters to His Son Lucien.* London, 1943, pp. 22-23. Letter of February 28, 1883.

There followed a whole succession of exhibitions in London, Paris, Brussels, and Edinburgh, awards, sales, negotiations, and discussions in fashionable circles. The master began to have disciples, one of them Walter Sickert. Mrs. Cassatt, the sister-in-law of the Impressionist painter (who said, "It is a good thing to have a Whistler in the family"), commissioned a portrait, *Arrangement in Black No. 8.* But ever since his trial, he had been busy trying to confound his detractors and assert the right of any artist to paint as he feels. On February 20, 1885, Whistler gave a lecture entitled "The Ten O'Clock" (that was the time at which it was given) at Prince's Hall, but it did not convince his audience, and one or two remarks on the behavior of writers provoked Oscar Wilde's wrath and attracted Swinburne's spite. Three years later Mallarmé, who had probably met Whistler at Manet's studio as a result of an introduction by Duret (unless it was Monet who introduced them over a formal lunch in Paris), agreed to translate the paper in French. Mallarmé, a Symbolist poet who was teaching English at the time, was the mentor of some of the best Modernist writers and artists. The Tuesday gatherings at his apartment on the Rue de Rome were famous.

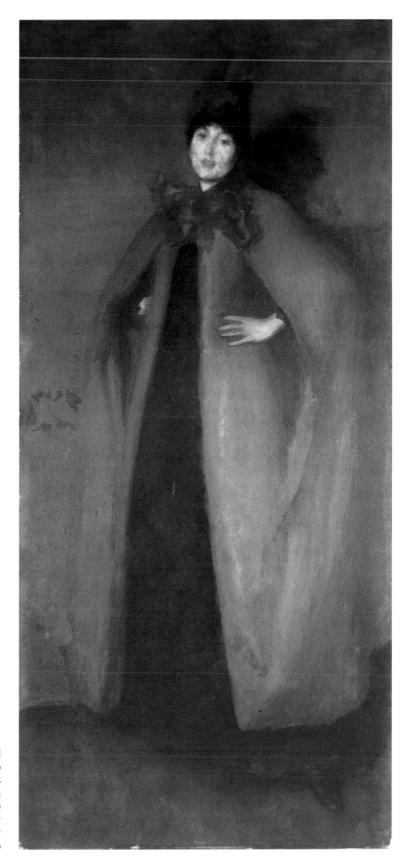

Harmony in Red
Lamplight, ca 1884-1886
Oil on canvas
190.5 × 89.7 cm
(76¾" × 35⅜")
Hunterian Art Gallery
University of Glasgow
Gift of Birnie Philip

Hôtel de Ville, Loches
1888
Etching, I/I
27 × 16.5 cm
(10⁹⁄₁₆" × 6⁷⁄₁₆")
National Gallery of Art
Washington, D.C.
Rosenwald Collection

Palaces, Brussels, 1887
Etching and
drypoint, I/II
21.7 × 13.8 cm
(8⁹⁄₁₆" × 5⁷⁄₁₆")
National Gallery of Art
Washington, D.C.
Rosenwald Collection

The Mill, 1889
Etching, I/IV
16 × 24 cm
(6 ⁵⁄₁₆" × 9 ½")
The Freer Gallery of Art
Smithsonian Institution
Washington, D.C.

44. Jacques-Emile
Blanche, *op.cit.*

WHISTLERISM COMES INTO ITS OWN

Jacques-Emile Blanche noted: "When we were young, Whistlerism and Mallarméism were labels that caught our fancy as preciosities worthy of us superior beings, and were also neologisms which made an impression on the public."[44] He called on Whistler in London in 1885. He later wrote an account of Whistler's apartment, the apartment of an aesthete; of the man himself, whom he did not like; and of the paintings, the portraits in particular, about which he wrote that Whistler "did not *finish* more than a dozen or so in his life." Then there were the sketches, "in which wan little figures in the Japanese girl mold, both affected and hieratic [words in vogue at the time], wave fans and parasols against sickly turquoise backgrounds." This savage attack goes on for several pages. Only the portraits of Lady Meux find favor with Blanche, who, praising them, confessed that never had he had such a revelation of a new art.

The Dancer
Green and Blue, ca 1890
Watercolor on blue ground
26.6 × 17.2 cm
(10 ½" × 6 ¾")
Private collection
U.S.A.

A warm friendship developed between Whistler and Mallarmé, the poet famed for his predilection for the rare and the recondite. His translation of the "Ten O'Clock" lecture appeared first in the "Revue indépendante" in May 1888 and later in a pamphlet which the author dedicated "to Degas, charming enemy and best of friends." It was read aloud at Berthe Morisot's salon. The critics seized

The Embroidered Curtain
1889
Etching, IV/VII
23.9 × 16 cm
(9 7/16" × 6 5/16")
The Freer Gallery of Art
Smithsonian Institution
Washington, D.C.

Stormy Sunset. Venice, 1889
Pastel on brown paper
18.5 × 28.3 cm
(7 ¼" × 11 ⅛")
Fogg Art Museum, Harvard University, Cambridge Massachusetts. Bequest of Grenville L. Winthrop

upon it, especially Huysmans, who enthused over the *Nocturnes* exhibited at the Durand-Ruel Gallery: "Veiled horizons half seen in another world [...] a spectacle of blurred nature or floating cities [...] bathed in the uncertain light of a dream." He also praised Whistler for having "aristocratically practiced an art impenetrable to the received ideas and aloof from the common herd, an art withdrawn in splendid isolation and proud reserve." The "Ten O'Clock de M. Whistler" was a constant subject of discussion in salons, cafés, and studios, and above all at the Tuesday gatherings held at Mallarmé's apartment. It is true that Whistlerism and Mallarméism, whether they were seductive poisons, exotic opiates, or overelaborate artworks, caused excitement, annoyance, or outright rebellion in the years of Symbolism.

In 1888, Whistler suddenly broke off with Maud Franklin, thereby creating further trouble for himself, and in August he married Beatrix Godwin, the wealthy widow of his friend E.W. Godwin, the architect. After the honeymoon, they

The Winged Hat, 1890
Lithograph
17.8 × 17 cm (7" × 6¾")
The Metropolitan Museum
of Art, New York
Harris Brisbane Dick Fund

moved to 110 Rue du Bac, and he took up a studio in the Rue Notre-Dame-des-Champs.   He was awarded the Legion of Honor.   He became in Paris a rallying point for the aesthetes and snobs of the day, as he had previously been in London.

In 1891, after organized lobbying by Mallarmé and the influential critics Duret, Gustave Geffroy and Roger Marx, the *Portrait of the Painter's Mother* was purchased for the Musée du Luxembourg.   A number of well-known contemporaries regarded it as one of the masterpieces of the century.   This official recognition had a welcome effect on Whistler's reputation in both Britain and the United States.   Shortly before, the Corporation of Glasgow acquired his *Portrait of Thomas Carlyle*.   His retrospective exhibition of forty-three *Nocturnes*, *Marines* and *Chevalet Pieces*, held at the Goupil Gallery in London in March 1892, was highly successful.

When he was not writing a malicious lampoon or giving a sensational interview, living down spiteful gossip about his break with Maud Franklin and his marriage, or entertaining, perorating, or publishing a miscellany of pieces including a selection of his correspondence ("The Gentle Art of Making Enemies") and an account of the Ruskin libel suit 'which delighted Mallarmé, Whistler occasionally found time to organize an exhibition, work on prints, and paint.   Montesquiou

The Rose Scarf, ca 1890
Oil on panel
25.8 × 18 cm (10⅛" × 7")
Hunterian Art Gallery
University of Glasgow
Gif of Birnie Philip

Portrait of Mallarmé
1892
Lithograph
9.9 × 7 cm (3⅞" × 2¾")
National Gallery of Art
Washington, D.C.
Rosenwald Collection

was among his fashionable friends and admirers, praising his talents to the skies on both sides of the Channel.   Whistler painted his portrait, *Arrangement in Black and Gold*.   Unfortunately, it is too conventional a painting, a tame portrait which fails to suggest the flamboyant and effete staginess of the man.   However, Montesquiou left a hilarious account of the portrait sittings which has the two narcissistic creatures face to face and one saying to the other, "Look at me another moment and you will look at yourself for ever!"   By contrast the small lithograph portrait of Mallarmé is astonishingly true to life.   Produced in 1893 in the Rue du Bac studio, after a few preliminary studies, it appeared as a frontispiece to "Vers et Prose".   As Duret wrote later, "The Mallarmé is extraordinarily lifelike.   [...] Anyone who knew him can almost hear him speak."   The poet himself was delighted with it.

Arrangement in Black and
Gold. Comte Robert
de Montesquiou-Fezensac
1891-1892
Oil on canvas
208.6 × 91.88 cm
(82⅛" × 36⅛")
The Frick Collection
New York

Mr. and Mrs. Whistler went on a tour of Britanny.   When they returned to Paris they entertained on a large scale (their Sunday brunches were famous).   At these gatherings Whistler would always be conspicuous, dressed in extravagant outfits with outrageous neckties.   The walls would be painted yellow, and there would always be a profusion of baubles to gaze at, including his precious blue and white porcelain.   These were the decadent Nineties, with the superficial Symbolism of Huysmans and Jean Lorrain.   Yet Whistler's real aspirations were elsewhere.   He dreamed to escape from what he considered to be the vulgarity and banality of the world he lived in.   The setting of his life, his poseur's existence, acted as a smoke screen.   His artificial entourage of snobs and flatterers was only a puppet theater under his disillusioned eye.   One person who understood Whistler was Mallarmé.   He recognized the depth in this aggressive society man with a sensuous temperament.   Whistler appreciated Mallarmé's taste for nocturnes, for mystery and silence, and he sensed that Mallarmé was a self-protected but painfully sensitive man — a poet of the dreamy suggestion, for whom art had an evocative power beyond the everyday significance of things.   Their friendship, which lasted until Mallarmé's death, is attested to by a moving exchange of correspondence.

What Whistler perhaps lacked was stronger creative impulse and the belief in the discipline required to go beyond the initial impression made by the shifting scene when contours fade and night begins to fall.   This shortcoming may partly explain the frustration that came through in his recurrent bouts of bad temper.   He gave himself up to the pleasure of the moment and was oblivious to the passing of time.   As Proust was to write of Elstir, "His efforts had gone toward dissolving that collocation of judgment which we call vision," and this phrase sums up Whistler's approach quite well.   It explains why his small-scale works, and those done on the spur of the moment, are sometimes more spirited than his larger compositions.   But in his etchings, the immediacy of his images reveals him as a master.

He stopped accepting commissions for portraits, but the one he did of himself, dating from 1895-1900, is terrifying.   Is the hesitant shadow of a man staring there out of the darkness really the hawk-eyed dandy who once strutted in the glare of publicity, assailed by admirers of both sexes in Paris and London? Is this the perfect arbiter of taste, the representative of a new order of nobility which Degas had acidly dismissed as "Art killed by Taste"?   Is this the man whom Helleu, no doubt involuntarily, caricatured at about the same time as an old lion with a monocle and a bristling forelock, his fingers curved against his brow and his eyes half-closed, his transformation into Elstir almost complete?...

Between 1890 and 1900, Whistler painted young women or adolescent girls with slightly sad or pensive faces: Miss Ethel Philip (*Harmony in Black*),[45] Miss Kinsella (*Rose and Green: The Iris*),[46] Alice Butt, Geneviève Mallarmé (*Rose and Gray*), *The Little Rose of Lyme Regis*,[47] a charming picture of a girl with a prettily sulky expression whose name was Rosie Randall, painted at a resort near Dorset where Whistler's wife was staying because of illness.   *Rose and Gold: Pretty Nelly Brown* and *Brown and Gold: Lillie in Our Valley*[48] are no less remarkable, but they betray Whistler's increasing anxiety.   Unfortunately, he was overdiluting his paints in spirits, so that a number of these paintings have lost their original freshness.   The reason for his worry was that Beatrix — Trixie — was dying of cancer.   The couple moved several times, and Whistler tried to keep his mind occupied by painting Pompeian nudes or doing scenes of his beloved Thames and the Waterloo

45. Hunterian Art Gallery, University of Glasgow.

46. Virginia Steele Scott Foundation, Pasadena, California.

47. Museum of Fine Arts, Boston.

48. Fogg Art Museum, Harvard University, Cambridge, Massachusetts.

Brown and Gold
Self-Portrait, 1895-1900
Oil on canvas
95.8 × 51.5 cm
(37 ⅝" × 20 ¼")
Hunterian Art Gallery
University of Glasgow
Gift of Birnie Philip

docks in paints or lithographs. He became increasingly irritable, embarking on a new court case (over inadequate payment for a portrait), attacking one critic or another for some real or imagined slight, and fell out with old friends.

There was scarcely another artist living at the turn of the century whose fame was such in Britain or France, or especially in the United States, where his works fetched enormous prices. His chief patron, Charles Lang Freer, a rich Detroit manufacturer, set up the most important collection of his work at what is now the Freer Gallery in Washington, D.C. Whistler painted Freer's portrait in 1902-1903.

After Trixie's death on May 10, 1896, Whistler became a mere shadow of his former self. His portraits of women and young girls and his landscapes — particularly seascapes of the violent surf at Pourville-sur-Mer near Dieppe — are scarcely more than attractive exercises in his late manner, painted with bravura and fineness unaffected by age. As a way of taking his mind off his grief he traveled around the Mediterranean, kept himself busy with litigation, and even opened an art school, the Académie Carmen, in the Passage Stanislas in Paris. However, his constant comings and goings between London and Paris meant frequent absences, and his pupils lost interest. The academy closed its doors in 1901. On September 9, 1898, Mallarmé died. "I have been exiled from the Rue de Rome for a century," Whistler had written rather sadly a few

The Sisters, 1894
Lithograph, II/II
15 × 23 cm
(5 ¹⁵⁄₁₆" × 9 ¹⁄₁₆")
The Freer Gallery of Art
Smithsonian Institution
Washington, D.C.

Miss Ethel Philip, 1894
Oil on panel
21.3 × 12.7 cm
(8⅜" × 5")
Hunterian Art Gallery
University of Glasgow
Gift of Birnie Philip

"La Fruitière de la Rue
de Grenelle", 1894
Lithograph
22.7 × 15.5 cm
(9" × 6⅛")
The Metropolitan Museum
of Art, New York
Harris Brisbane Dick Fund

Rose and Brown
The Philosopher
(Edward Halloway)
1896-1897
Oil on panel
21.5 × 13.5 cm
(8⅜" × 5¼")
Private Collection

By the Balcony, 1896
Lithograph
21.3 × 14 cm
(8½" × 5½")
The Metropolitan Museum
of Art, New York
Harris Brisbane Dick Fund

months earlier. In "Divagations. Quelques médaillons et portraits en pied" of 1897, Mallarmé had praised Whistler "the conjurer of a work of mystery enclosed in its perfection." By that time Whistler's own health was faltering.

Whistler's last honor was to be elected the first president of the International Society of Sculptors, Painters and Engravers, whose first exhibition was held in Knightsbridge, in London in May 1898. His works were shown there alongside

"La Belle Dame Endormie"
1896
Lithograph, 19.8 × 15.5 cm
(7¾" × 6⅛")
The Freer Gallery of Art
Smithsonian Institution
Washington, D.C.

those of Manet, Monet, Toulouse-Lautrec, Sisley, Max Liebermann, Bonnard, and Vuillard. At the Second International Exhibition at Knightsbridge the following year, a whole room was dedicated to his prints. That same year, at Sergei Diaghilev's invitation, Whistler took part in the World of Art Exhibition, in St. Petersburg, which presented the European and Russian avant-garde. The famous Russian collector Sergei Shchukin, who was later to assemble a remarkable collection of paintings by Henri Matisse and Pablo Picasso, bought a number of works from him. But Whistler was past his time. He took an interest in Art Nouveau, of which he had been a precursor, and subscribed to "Ver Sacrum", the magazine of the Viennese Secession. His drawings after the dancer Loie Fuller show that he was intrigued by the swirling lines of the Liberty style.

In his last works, Whistler dwelt on the faded colors of old, dilapidated shopfronts, in paintings like *A Shop in Calais* of 1896, or *The Laundress, Dieppe* of 1899, or in hazy landscapes such *The Dome in the Distance*, painted in Ajaccio in 1901,[49] or *Marseilles, Harbor*, also of 1901. The flat colors, tonalities in a minor key so to speak, with their muted effects of old rose and faded green and ocher, bring to mind paintings by Edouard Vuillard and Pierre Bonnard.

Whistler died in London on July 17, 1903, at the height of his fame, which was equal to that of Manet, Degas, or Renoir. Nevertheless, despite some impressive portraits and some delicate landscapes, his late work had betrayed certain weaknesses. It was as much the prophet of modernity as the arbiter of taste who was acclaimed. This must explain why his direct influence was limited, apart from certain affinities of style among young artists, mainly in the English speaking world, and some of his distinctive effects of composition or atmosphere. James McNeill Whistler stands alone, an isolated case. That closes the discussion but it leaves his wider place in history unresolved.

PIERRE CABANNE

Pantheon, Luxembourg Gardens, 1892-1893
Etching, I/I
8.3 × 19.8 cm
(3 ¼" × 7 ⅞")
The Freer Gallery of Art
Smithsonian Institution
Washington, D.C.

49. The three paintings are at the Hunterian Art Gallery, University of Glasgow.

Dorothy Seton
A Daughter of Eve, 1903
Oil on canvas
51.7 × 31.8 cm
(19 ⅞" × 12 ½")
Hunterian Art Gallery
University of Glasgow
Gift of Birnie Philip

1834   James Abbott Whistler was born on July 11, at Lowell, Massachusetts.

1843   The family moved to St. Petersburg.

1848   Because of bouts of rheumatic fever, he spent most of the year with his older half-sister, who was married to Seymour Haden, a surgeon and an accomplished engraver.

1849   The family returned to the United States after his father died. First known painting: *The Artist's Niece.*

1851   Arrived at West Point on June 3. Dismissed in 1853.

1852   Admitted to the drawing classes conducted at West Point by Robert Weir.

1854   Lengthy stay in Baltimore with the family of Tom Winans, a wealthy industrialist. Whistler spent his time sketching in the drawing office of the Winans locomotive factory. Received an appointment with the United States Coast Survey Office, where he took his first lessons in etching.

1855   Resigned on February 12. Winans encouraged him in his artistic ambitions and assisted him with loans for materials. A few portraits. Arrived in Paris on November 3.

1856   Bohemian life. Entered the Académie Gleyre. Copied paintings at the Louvre.

1857   In September, went to see the Manchester Art Treasures exhibition, where he could see an outstanding selection of Dutch 17th-century paintings and etchings.

1858   First series of etchings. Returned to Paris in April, where he began etchings of working women in the Realist vein. Traveled through Alsace and the Rhineland to Amsterdam. Met Fantin-Latour who introduced him to Legros, Bracquemond and Manet. *At the Piano.*

1859   *At the Piano* was rejected by the Salon. Several trips to London, where two etchings were exhibited. Etchings on the Thames, first drypoints.

1860   Set up a studio in London. *Wapping on Thames, The Thames in Ice, Harmony in Green and Rose: The Music Room. At the Piano* was exhibited at the Royal Academy. Jo Hiffernan became his mistress and model.

1861   Seascapes in Britanny. Met Degas.

1862   Moved to Chelsea. *Symphony in White No. 1. The White Girl* was rejected by the Royal Academy. Seascapes of the Basque coast. Beginning of his friendship with Dante Gabriel Rossetti.

1863   *The White Girl* at the Salon des Refusés. Ceased to etch for seven years. Trip to Amsterdam.

1864   *La Princesse du Pays de la Porcelaine.* Japonesque inspiration. Rossetti introduced him to Frederick Leyland, a Liverpool shipping magnate.

1865   Trip on the Rhine, followed by a stay at Trouville with Courbet. Seascapes. *Symphony in White No. 2* was exhibited at the Royal Academy. Met Albert Moore.

1866   Trip to Chile. Views of Valparaiso and first night scenes.

1867   Night scenes on the Thames. Break with Haden and Legros.

1868   First visit to Speke Hall, Leyland's residence in Liverpool.

1871   Publication of the *Thames Set. Portrait of the Painter's Mother,* which was reluctantly accepted the following year by the committee for the Royal Academy.

1872   *Portrait of Thomas Carlyle.* First series of *Nocturnes.*

1874   First one-man show at the Flemish Gallery in London. Portraits and *Nocturnes. Nocturne in Black and Gold: The Falling Rocket.*

1875-1876 Etchings and drypoints of scenes on the Thames.

1876   Took part in the exhibition of the Société des Artistes Français at the Deschamps Gallery in London. *The Peacock Room.* Maud Franklin became his mistress and model.

1877   Break with Leyland. Disastrous libel suit against the art critic John Ruskin.

1878   First lithographs.

1879   Etchings of the Thames. Was declared bankrupt in spite of the commercial success of his etchings. He lost his house in London and his art collection was auctioned off. The Fine Art Society commissioned 12 etchings of Venice. Left for Venice in September.

1880   Etchings and pastels of Venice. Back in London, he published the first *Venice Set,* 12 etchings which were not well received by the public and the critics.

1881   Exhibited 53 pastels of Venice at the Fine Art Society. Etchings and pastels of London. His mother died.

1883   Exhibited 51 etchings of Venice and London at the Fine Art Society. The show was a critical failure but was greatly admired by such artists as Millais and Pissarro. Took part in the 2nd International Exhibition at the Georges Petit Gallery in Paris. *Portrait of Théodore Duret.* Landscapes in oils and watercolors in Wales. Lithographs.

1884   Major one-man show of watercolors at the Dowdeswell Gallery in London.

1885   Delivered his "The Ten O'Clock" lecture in London. Traveled to Belgium, Holland, and Dieppe.

1886   Published the second *Venice Set.* In June, he was elected president of the Society of British Artists, an exhibition society created to break the monopoly of the Royal Academy. One-man show at the Dowdeswell Gallery in London: *Notes, Harmonies* and *Nocturnes.*

1887   Published the *Jubilee Set,* 12 small etchings. Traveled to Belgium and Holland in the fall. Took part in the 6th International Exhibition at the Georges Petit Gallery. Published six lithographs, *Art Notes.*

1888   Published 19 etchings, 13 of Brussels. He married Beatrix Goodwin. Trip to the Loire valley and the towns of the Touraine: *Renaissance etchings,* which were never published as a set. Took part in the International Exhibition in Munich. Mallarmé translated his "Ten O'Clock". Duret published "Whistler et son œuvre".

1889 Major exhibition of oils, watercolors and pastels at the Wunderlich Gallery in New York. Trip to Amsterdam in August: 10 etchings which were exhibited the following year in New York and London and greatly admired by Bernard Shaw.

1890-1896 Lithographs.

1890 Met Charles Lang Freer, an industrialist from Detroit and a patron of the arts. He owned the largest collection of works by Whistler. Published his correspondence, "The Gentle Art of Making Enemies".

1891 *Portrait of the Painter's Mother* was purchased for the French National Collection (4,000 Francs). *Portrait of Robert de Montesquiou.*

1892 Retrospective exhibition at the Goupil Gallery in London. Settled in Paris at 110 Rue du Bac, with a studio at 86 Rue Notre-Dame-des-Champs. Awarded the Legion of Honor. Etchings of Paris. Took part in the 2nd exhibition of the Société Nationale des Beaux-Arts in Paris and the 6th International Exhibition in Munich.

1893 Abandoned etching in favor of lithographs: 12 prints of Paris subjects. Trip to Britanny in July.

1894 His wife was stricken with cancer. Series of nudes and portraits.

1895 Portraits of young women and children. Self-portraits. Stay at Lyme Regis, Dorset.

1896 Abandoned lithography after his wife's death.

1897 *Rose and Gray: Geneviève Mallarmé.* Stay at Dieppe.

1898 Elected president of the International Society of Sculptors, Painters and Engravers. He opened a short-lived art school in Paris, 6 Passage Stanislas.

1899 Stay in Rome and Florence. Summer at Pourville-sur-Mer. His etchings were given a special room at the 2nd International Exhibition at Knightsbridge in London. Traveled to Holland and to Ireland.

1900 Winter in London and part of the summer in Ireland. Traveled to Gibraltar, Tangiers and Algiers. Was awarded the Grand Prix for etching at the World Fair in Paris.

1901 Fell ill in Marseilles. Stay in Corsica, where he resumed etching. Returned to London in May and sold his house in Paris. Stay at Bath.

1902 Traveled to Holland with Charles Freer.

1903 Died of a heart attack in London on July 17. He was buried in a little churchyard in Chiswick.

1905 Major retrospective exhibitions at the New Gallery in London (750 works) and at the École des Beaux-Arts in Paris (438 works).

Cremorne Gardens No. 2, 1872-1877
Oil on canvas, 68.6 × 134.9 cm (27" × 53 ⅛")
The Metropolitan Museum of Art, New York
John Stewart Kennedy Fund

SELECTED BIBLIOGRAPHY

CATALOGUES RAISONNÉS

KENNEDY, Edward G. *The Etched Work of Whistler. Illustrated by reproductions in collotype of the different states of the plates.* New York: Grolier Club, 1910. Reprint, San Francisco: Alan Wofsy, 1978.

KENNEDY, Edward G. *The Lithographs of Whistler. Illustrated by reproductions in photogravure and lithograph, arranged according to the catalogue by Thomas R. Way with additional subjects not before recorded.* New York, 1914.

LEVY, Mervyn and STALEY, Allen. *Whistler Lithographs: A Catalogue Raisonné.* London: Jupiter, 1975.

MACDONALD, Margaret F. *James McNeill Whistler: Drawings, Pastels and Watercolours, A Catalogue Raisonné.* New Haven, Conn., London: Yale University Press, 1994.

MANSFIELD, Howard. *A Descriptive Catalogue of the Etchings and Drypoints of James McNeill Whistler.* Chicago, 1904.

YOUNG, Andrew McLaren, MACDONALD, Margaret F., SPENCER, Robin and MILES, Hamish. *The Paintings of James McNeill Whistler.* 2 vols. New Haven, Conn., London: Yale University Press.

WRITINGS BY WHISTLER

The Gentle Art of Making Enemies. London: Heinemann, 1890. 2nd ed., London, New York, 1892 (with the catalogue of *Nocturnes, Marines & Chevalet Pieces* and five other letters). Reprint, New York: G.P. Putnam's, 1953.

Eden versus Whistler: The Baronet and the Butterfly. A Valentine with a Verdict. Paris, New York, 1899.

BOOKS

BACHER, Otto. *With Whistler in Venice.* New York: The Century Co., 1908.

BARBIER, Carl P., ed. *Correspondance Mallarmé-Whistler.* Paris, 1964.

BECKER, Eugene Matthew. *Whistler and the Aesthetic Movement.* Unpublished Ph.D. dissertation, Princeton University, 1959. Ann Arbor, Mich.: UMI, 1979.

BELL, Nancy R.E. *James McNeill Whistler.* London, 1905.

BÉNÉDITE, Léonce. *L'Œuvre de James McNeill Whistler.* Paris: Gazette des Beaux-Arts, 1905.

BERGER, Klaus. *Japonismus in der westlichen Malerei.* Munich, 1980.

BLANCHE, Jacques-Emile. *De David à Degas.* Paris, 1927.

BOWDOIN, W.G. *James McNeill Whistler. The Man and His Work.* London 1902.

CARY, Elizabeth Luther. *The Works of James McNeill Whistler: A Study, with a Tentative List of the Artist's Works.* New York: Moffat, Yard & Co., 1907.

CHISABURO, Yamada, ed. *Japonisme in Art: An International Symposium.* Tokyo: Committee for the Year 2001 and Kodansha Int. Ltd., 1981.

DOGSON, Campbell. *The Etchings of James McNeill Whistler.* London: Studio Ltd., 1922.

DUFWA, Jacques. *Winds from the East: A Study in the Art of Manet Degas Monet and Whistler 1856-86.* Stockholm: Almqist & Wiksell. Atlantic Highlands, N.J.: Humanities Press, 1981.

DU MAURIER, Daphne, ed. *The Young George Du Maurier: A Selection of His Letters 1860-67.* London, 1951.

DURET, Théodore. *Histoire de James McNeill Whistler et son œuvre.* Paris: Floury, 1904. Trans. by Frank Rutter. London: G. Richards Ltd. Philadelphia: Lippincott, 1917.

EDDY, Arthur J. *Recollections and Impressions of James McNeill Whistler.* Philadelphia, London: 1903, 1904.

FLEMING, Gordon. *The Young Whistler 1834-1866.* London, Boston: Allen & Unwin, 1978.

GALLATIN, Albert E. *Whistler's Dicta and Other Essays.* Boston, 1904.

GALLATIN, Albert E. *Whistler's: Notes and Footnotes and Other Memoranda.* New York, 1907.

GALLATIN, Albert E. *Portraits and Caricatures of James McNeill Whistler, an Iconoaraphy.* London, New York, Toronto: Lane, 1913.

GALLATIN, Albert E. *Portraits of Whistler: A Critical Study and an Iconography.* London, New York, Toronto: Lane, 1918.

GETSCHER, Robert, H. *Whistler and Venice.* Unpublished Ph.D. dissertation, Case Western Reserve University, Cleveland, 1970. Ann Arbor, Mich.: UMI, 1974.

GETSCHER, Robert, H. *James Abbott McNeill Whistler. Pastels.* New York, 1991.

GETSCHER, Robert, H. and MARKS, Paul G. *James McNeill Whistler and John Singer Sargent.* New York, London, 1986.

GORDER, Judith Elaine. *James McNeill Whistler: A Study of the Oil Paintings, 1855-69.* Unpublished Ph.D. dissertation, University of Iowa, 1973. Ann Arbor, Mich.: UMI, 1974.

GREGORY, Horace. *The World of James McNeill Whistler.* New York: Nelson, 1959.

HOLDEN, Donald. *Whistler Landscapes and Seascapes.* New York: Watson-Guptill, 1959.

LANE, James Warren. *Whistler.* New York, 1942.

LAVER, James. *Whistler.* London: Faber & Faber, 1930, 1951.

LOCHNAN, Katharine A. *Whistler's Etchings and the Sources of His Etching Style 1855-80.* Unpublished Ph.D. dissertation, Courtauld Institute, London University, 1982.

MACDONALD, Margaret. *Whistler and Mallarmé.* Oxford: Clarendon Press, 1959.

MCMULLEN, Roy. *Victorian Outsider. A Biography of James McNeill Whistler.* New York: Dutton, 1973.

MAUCLAIR, Camille. *De Watteau à Whistler.* Paris, 1905.

MENPES, Mortimer. *Whistler as I knew Him.* London: Adam & Charles Black, 1904.

MERRILL, Linda. *A Pot of Paint: Aesthetics on Trial in Whistler v. Ruskin.* Washington, D.C., London, 1992.

MUMFORD, Elizabeth. *Whistler's Mother.* Boston, 1939.

NAYLOR, Maria. *Selected Etchings of James McNeill Whistler.* New York: Dover, 1975.

Parry, Albert. *Whistler's Father*. New York: Bobbs-Merrill, 1939.

Pearson, Hesketh. *The Man Whistler*. London: Methuen, 1952. New York: Taplinger, 1978.

Pennell, Elizabeth Robins. *Whistler the Friend*. Philadelphia: Lippincott, 1930.

Pennell, Elizabeth Robins and Pennell, Joseph. *The Life of James McNeill Whistler*. 2 vols. Philadelphia: Lippincott. London: Heinemann, 1908.

Pennell, Elizabeth Robins and Pennell, Joseph. *The Whistler Journal*. Philadelphia: Lippincott, 1921.

Pousette-Dart, Nathaniel. *James McNeill Whistler*. New York, 1924.

Prideaux, Tom. The World of Whistler. New York, 1970.

Rutter, Frank. *James McNeill Whistler. An Estimate and a Biography*. London: Grant Richards; New York: M. Kennerley, 1911.

Seitz, Don Carlos. *Whistler Stories*. New York, London: Harper & Brothers, 1913.

Sickert, Bernhard. *Whistler*. London: Duckworth, 1908.

Spencer, Robin. *James McNeill Whistler and His Circle*. Unpublished M.A. report, Courtauld Institute, London University, 1968.

Spencer, Robin. *The Aesthetic Movement*. New York, 1972.

Spencer, Robin, ed. *Whistler: A Retrospective*. New York, 1989.

Sutton, Denys. *Nocturne. The Art of James McNeill Whistler* Philadelphia: Lippincott, 1963.

Sutton, Denys. *James McNeill Whistler. Paintings, Etchings, Pastels and Watercolours*. London: Phaidon, 1966.

Taylor, Hilary. *James McNeill Whistler*. New York: G.P. Putnam's, 1978.

Thomas, Ralph. *A Catalogue of the Etchings and Drypoints of J.A.M. Whistler*. London: J.R. Smith, 1874.

Way, Thomas R. *Mr. Whistler's Lithographs: The Catalogue*. London, 1896. London, New York, 1905.

Way, Thomas R. *Memories of James McNeill Whistler, the Artist*. London, New York, 1912.

Way, Thomas R. and Dennis, G.R. *The Art of James McNeill Whistler*. London: George Bell & Sons, 1903.

Wedmore, Sir Frederick. *Whistler's Etchings. A Study and Catalogue*. London, 1886.

Weintraub, Stanley. *Whistler. A Biography*. New York: Weybright & Talley, 1974.

Weisberg, Gabriel P., ed. *Japonisme: Japanese Influence on French Art 1854-1910*. Cleveland, Ohio: Cleveland Museum of Art, 1975.

EXHIBITIONS SINCE 1951

1951   *Whistler. Arrangements in Grey and Black*. Art Gallery and Museum, Kelvingrove, Glasgow. Catalogue by T.J. Honeyman.

1954   *Etchings, Dry-Points and Lithographs by Whistler*. The Arts Council of Great Britain, London.
Sargent, Whistler, and Mary Cassatt. The Art Institute, Chicago. The Metropolitan Museum of Art, New York. Catalogue by Frederick A. Sweet.

1960   *James McNeill Whistler: An Exhibitions of Paintings and Other Works*. The Art Council of Great Britain, London. Knoedler Galleries, New York. Catalogue by Andrew McLaren Young.

1968   *ames McNeill Whistler: Paintings, Pastels, Watercolors, Etchings, Lithographs*. The Art Institute, Chicago. The Munson William Proctor Institute, Utica, New York. Catalogue by Frederick A. Sweet.

1969   *James McNeill Whistler*. Nationalgalerie Staatliche Museen, Berlin. Catalogue by Robin Spencer.

1971   *From Realism to Symbolism: Whistler and His World*. Wildenstein & Co., New York. Philadelphia Museum of Art. Catalogue by Allen Staley *et al*.

1976   *Whistler, the Graphic Work: Amsterdam, Liverpool, London, Venice*. T. Agnew & Sons Ltd., London. Walker Art Gallery, Liverpool. Glasgow Art Gallery and Museum. Catalogue by Margaret MacDonald.

1977   *The Stamp of Whistler* Allen Memorial Art Museum, Oberlin Ohio. Catalogue by Robert H. Getscher.

1978   *Whistler: Themes and Variations*. Montgomery Art Gallery, Pomona College, Claremont, Cal. Crocker Art Gallery, Sacramento, Cal. Stanford University Art Museum, Cal.
Whistler: The Later Years. University of Michigan Museum of Art, Ann Arbor.

1980   *Whistler's and Further Family*. Glasgow University Library. Catalogue by Kate Donally and Nigel Thorp.

1983   *A Cultivated Taste. Whistler and American Print Collectors*. Davison Art Center, Wesleyan University, Middletown, Conn. Catalogue by M. Lee Wiehl.
La Femme. The Influence of Whistler and Japanese Print Masters on American Art, 1880-1917. Grand Central Art Galleries, New York. Catalogue by Gary Levine, Robert R. Preato and Francine Tyler.

1984   *Whistler Pastels*. Hunterian Art Gallery, University of Glasgow. Catalogue by Margaret MacDonald.
Notes, Harmonies, Nocturnes. M. Knoedler & Co., New York. Catalogue by Margaret MacDonald.
Drawing Near: Whistler Etchings from the Zelman Collection. Los Angeles county Museum of Art. The National Gallery, Washington, D.C. Catalogue by Ruth Fine.
The Etchings of James McNeill Whistler. The Metropolitan Museum of Art, New York. The Art Gallery of Ontario, Toronto. Catalogue by Katharine A. Lochnan.
James McNeill Whistler at the Freer Gallery of Art. Freer Gallery of Art, Washington, D.C. Catalogue by David Park Curry.

1987   *Whistler graveur*. Musée d'Orsay, Paris.

1987-1988 *James McNeill Whistler*. Isetan Museum of Art, Tokyo. Hokkaido Museum of Modern Art, Sapporo. Shizuoka Prefectural Museum. Daimaru Museum, Osaka. Catalogue by M. Hopkinson *et al*.

1994-1995 *James McNeill Whistler*. Tate Gallery, London. Musée d'Orsay, Paris. National Gallery of Art, Washington, D.C. Catalogue by Richard Dorment and Margaret MacDonald.

TABLE DES ILLUSTRATIONS